HOT IN THE POT

A Survival Guide for the *Real You* in
the Corporate World

by
Sharon Hoyle Weber

Hot in the Pot
A Survival Guide for the Real You *in the Corporate World*

iUniverse books may be ordered through booksellers or by contacting:

iUniverse
1663 Liberty Drive
Bloomington, IN 47403
www.iuniverse.com
1-800-Authors (1-800-288-4677)

Because of the dynamic nature of the Internet, any Web
addresses or links contained in this book may have changed
since publication and may no longer be valid.

ISBN: 978-0-595-44676-6 (pbk)
ISBN: 978-0-595-88999-0 (ebk)

Printed in the United States of America

Book cover image by Cindy Procious
Author photo by James Tringale

To Steve, Kyle, Gillian,
and all the Thrivers who have
inspired me and guided this book.

Contents

PART III

Introduction

I've spent fourteen years in conference rooms all over the country as a corporate trainer working with employees from staff to partners about how to work best together. I've taught everything from customer service, business development, and leadership to project management, and the list goes on and on. Through my relationship with Forum Corporation and Results by Design, I have worked with thousands of folks from companies such as Deloitte, Liberty Mutual, Hasbro Toys, and Bank of America. As much as I love being a corporate training facilitator, it means lots of travel and uncertainty about where my next paycheck is coming from.

A while back, a client asked me to take over a managerial position while they were recruiting for someone to take the position permanently. I was thrilled by the idea of four months of solid work without having to get on an airplane.

Everything was exciting about the first day at my new job: riding the commuter boat, feeling important as I swiped my badge through security, and seeing the big "Welcome, Sharon!" sign on my cubicle signed by all my new colleagues. I arrived like a kid on the first day of school playing office, setting up my desk, getting acquainted with the computer system, and scheduling all my on-boarding meetings. My job was to act as liaison between the contract employees and the firm. This had gone neglected for a while, and, having been a contract employee myself, I was full of great ideas.

As the weeks passed, I began to sense something was off. It wasn't anything in particular, just walking by cubicles the size of horse stalls, the mind-numbing office chitchat, and the endless "occasion" parties. I began feeling deflated, my spirit hissing out of me.

The physical space didn't help. The floor was a maze of beige cubicles and corporate "art." One day bleeding into the next with a stream of meetings, meetings to debrief meetings, meetings to decide on more meetings … so much talking, so little to show for it.

I was getting reacquainted with many people I had worked with over the years as a contract facilitator. Judging from the looks of some of them, cubicle life seems to accelerate the aging process. One woman I had worked with a few years earlier looked twice her age! She had gained weight and could have used a hair and wardrobe update. When I ran into those who had left and gone on their own, I noticed they looked ten years younger and had that twinkle in their eye and humor in their voice.

And what's with how people talk? "Let's set up a window of time to strategize a consistent and predictable response to the depletion of available and interested resources in the next quarter." Huh? Oh, we need people to do the job. Gotcha.

Everyone was so serious, no laughter, no energy, no enthusiasm.

It was really starting to affect me. The best part of me was leaking out little by little each day. I was tired and withdrawn. I can be fun at a party, but nobody at work would ever know it. A general malaise of emptiness and aimlessness hung over the office. I couldn't figure out what was sucking the life out of us. It was as if we were checking our souls at the revolving door.

I befriended a colleague who felt it, too. We would meet in those hidden corners where we couldn't be overheard and whisper about what was going on. She described it as the "Boiled Frog syndrome."

I asked, "What's that?"

She said, "If you want to boil a frog, not that anyone would, but if you did, and you tried to put it in a pot of boiling water, the frog would sense the danger and wiggle and squirm out of your hands. But if you put the frog into a pot of tepid water, it would swim happily. If you increased the temperature one degree at a time, the frog would adjust one degree at a time, never recognizing the point of danger. Sadly, it would boil to death."

That was me! I was that frog adapting to something that was sucking the *me* out of me. I was turning into a (doom music here) Corporate Boiled Frog.

During the change management movement in the early 1990s, the Boiled Frog analogy was used as a strategic tool, pointing out that companies could change anything as long as it was done gradually: demotions, reorganizations, policy changes, compensation depletion, all very sinister. But for me, it is a wake-up, shake-up call to all of us living a diluted existence during our many hours at work.

What exactly is a Boiled Frog at work? It is someone who hauls his or her self off to work every day, gradually becoming a mere shell of his or her *real* self, and has no clue it is happening. BF's are adapting one degree at a time to the Four P's: Pressures, Procedures, Policies, and Personalities. They get less and less satisfaction out of their work and feel more and more trapped by the income and benefits, thus caught in "the pot."

Sometimes BFs get so consumed by the stresses and demands of their jobs that they gradually stop taking care of themselves; they stop getting exercise, a haircut, picking up something to freshen up their wardrobe. The workweek drains so much out of them, they begin to feel indifferent to loved ones. They don't have the energy to make time to have fun or do the things they once enjoyed. With the pressures of living expenses, there doesn't seem to be any relief in sight.

Consider all the millions of us who work in the corporate world: mothers, brothers, aunts, husbands, neighbors. There is a collective spirit being diminished day in and day out. Imagine the impact on our families and communities! How different it would be if all the BF's felt alive, free, and energized—no matter what job they have. I began looking for people in the corporate world who aren't getting boiled, but are thriving. I call them *Thrivers:* people who make a good living, are learning and growing in their jobs, enjoy genuine relationships, look fresh, are healthy, have a sense of humor, and keep it all in perspective.

The first person I asked was a friend of mine who has been consulting in *Fortune* 1,500 companies for thirty years and has written a few business books. I asked if he knew anyone who fit my description. He responded, "No one comes to mind." Oh, great, do they even exist?

Well, eventually Thrivers did surface, and they knew other people. Soon I was interviewing Thrivers from various age groups, industries, roles, and incomes. The good news is that there *are* specific ways to thrive without getting boiled.

Having the opportunity to go in and out of so many *Fortune* 1,500 companies and talking with thousands of folks has made me see how the real self, the human spirit, is at risk in the halls and cubicles of the corporate world. In the following chapters, I share what I have learned after formally interviewing thirty Thrivers and talking with so many employees about how the real self thrives in the heat of the corporate pot. You will see what these folks say about how to have a *life* that *works*.

PART I

How Do You Become a Boiled Frog at Work? One Degree at a Time

… which is why it is so dangerous!

Each situation we face in which we compromise our real selves raises the temperature of the water. If a manager, client, or colleague asks us to lie or be phony in some drastic way, of course, we push back. However, how many of us are putting up with and shutting up about a policy we know is bull or worse, supporting it with our staff?

We need to be aware of the Four P's (Pressures, Procedures, Policies, and Personalities) that raise the temperature one degree at a time. It's the small daily battles "not worth fighting the system over" that boil the cool out of us. After four, ten, thirteen, twenty years, our true selves are barely breathing. What kind of compromises or concessions are you making day in and day out that are raising your temperature?

Here are a few stories of how a combination of the Four P's has boiled me, and my fellow BF's, that you may relate to.

Reduced

The incident that prompted this book and made me feel as if not only was I expected to wear beige and black on the outside, I was supposed to be beige and black on the inside too. It was a gray February day. I fought through the blistery wind from the commuter boat through the cold shadowy streets of Boston, mindlessly swiped my badge through security, and arrived at my beige cubicle. The phone mail light nagged me. I logged onto my computer and groaned at the slew of e-mails requesting things I didn't want to do. Ugh!

Tropical-colored Post-it notepads in all shapes and sizes were scattered on my desk. As I was listening to some long-winded phone mail messages, I picked up the stickies and started putting them onto my file cabinet making designs with them. This took on a life of its own.

By the end of the week, my cubicle was wallpapered in turquoise, fuchsia, and canary yellow Post-its that were bobbing and weaving all around my desk. The spray of color lifted my spirits and the spirits of those around me. I'd find notes saying, "Love your Post-its!" on my computer.

Some people even added to it. It was a harmless thing to do, since I only did it while listening to phone mail messages. The color was bringing me back to life. I was enjoying my job and feeling productive.

"It looks like someone is on psychedelic drugs in your office. Take 'em down," my manager spoke into my phone mail as my phone was cocked on my shoulder with Post-its in hand. "You haven't earned your right to be different," she said when I questioned why.

Problem with that is, by the time you've earned your right to be different, you aren't different anymore. I wish I could say I put up a big stink and started a revolution, but, for me, the job was a temporary position. I just grabbed my wastebasket and ripped them off.

In my manager's defense, companies have policies against my spray of color. Some organizations regulate how many personal items you can have in your space. But why?

I don't understand how it is a cost benefit to have employees check their most colorful selves at the door. Time and time again companies that start out in garages turn into huge organizations making tons of money, and they got that way with a maverick, irreverent spirit. Once they get so big, someone decides there's something to lose, and it all has to go. I'm watching to see what Google is going to do in the near future. Lewis Richmond, in his book, *Work as a Spiritual Practice,* says, "Jobs are not performed by robots." Sometimes it just feels like it.

Parboiled

Karin is an associate for a consulting firm. She is an assistant for the company library, which holds all the intellectual capital along with best practices, lessons learned, and the like. The intent is that the library will maximize efficiency with everyone learning from each other rather than reinventing the wheel or making the same mistakes over and over again. Karin, recently divorced, just returned to the workforce after bringing up a family of three. She is bright and articulate and arrived on the job very excited about her new life.

As she describes her story, it occurred to me that the process of how decisions are made heats up the water. Decisions that have an impact on how we do our jobs are made without our input, involvement, or even notification. Yet we are stuck with them no matter how stupid they may seem.

"When I first started this job, I was excited and scared. I loved what this company was doing, and I enjoyed being part of something that was leading edge," Karin says. "My manager and I hit it off right away, and we complement each other pretty well. She has a lot of exciting ideas and brings a lot of energy and vision to the work. I was very motivated to come to work." Karin was a classic frog slipping into the pot of tepid water and swimming about happily. She believed in the company and what they said they were all about.

"Then the organization started making decisions that made us feel like we were an afterthought, and they kept shuffling us around to different departments with different directors," she says. "At first, we were part of human resources with a great location and lots of support. Next thing we knew we were part of Technology and stuck in a closet somewhere. We kept having to adjust to a new director, which derailed us from achieving our goals." Starts and stops in productivity are unavoidable in any large corporation. But Karin and her team began losing the belief their work mattered.

She began seeing that what the company said and how it acted weren't adding up. If that wasn't bad enough, she recalls, "We were always the last to know; everyone else knew what was happening to our department weeks before we did. I saw what it did to my manager, and after that my productivity plummeted." It's embarrassing and demoralizing to be the last to know your department is getting tossed around like an old shoe.

Not surprisingly, she lost all trust. "I don't feel safe. Anything can happen. I no longer have any loyalty to this company."

Once, a happy frog, excited to go to work, engaged in the purpose of what she was doing, willing to give her all to see the effectiveness of the library evolve, Karin now shows up and goes through the motions, with her temperature rising.

Hard-boiled

The pressures of better, cheaper, faster can make it easy to forget who we are and what we really care about. Barbara, an ace project leader, is married, has no children, and is turning forty. By giving her job top priority for twelve years, Barbara was seduced into that all-familiar force of giving more time to her work and less to her personal life. For Barbara a strong ambition in a demanding job was a toxic cocktail. How did she finally become aware of what she was becoming?

"Two things happened within a short period of time that awakened me to what I had adapted to," Barbara told me. "First, my father was in the hospital with a serious illness, and I actually believed I didn't have time to go see him. The second was that a friend of mine, my age, discovered that he had cancer. Over the last year I spent a lot of time with him, and he passed away a few months ago. I thought to myself, if I were to die right now, what could I say about my life? That I ran a few good projects?"

Do we really need such dramatic alarms to snap us out of it? Sort of, because it happens so gradually, it's easy to miss the clues. Once Barbara awakened to what was taking place, more came to light. "I noticed subtle changes in my personality. I had become chronically tired and ill. I had no energy for anything. Everything I did, my entire focus, was my work. I discovered I don't like who I have become. I'm easily annoyed and angry. By how I behave, you would think I care more about budget and schedule than people. This is not me." Once she prioritized her job over everything else, Barbara was vulnerable to the ever-increasing demands and expectations of her colleagues and clients.

Laurie, once a senior accountant for a top-four accounting firm, can vouch for Barbara. "The more you do, the more work they give you," she says, "and now with the Sarbanes-Oxley [a new bill that regulates accounting practices that emerged after Enron], it's out of control." She, too, got caught up in the world of eighty-hour workweeks, but believes for her it was because she was a product of her experience. "I grew up in a low-income home in Buffalo, New York, in the 1960s and 1970s when there was 15 to 20 percent unemployment. To me, it is a badge of honor to have a job and make a good living."

Oftentimes circumstances at work make it easy for people like Laurie to overextend herself. She confesses that being so immersed in her work was a way to fulfill herself. Not fully understanding her own needs combined with her inability to set hard boundaries was like a *perfect storm*. "When I finally left, my body was still addicted to the adrenaline of the pace, and I suffered panic attacks," she remembers. "It took me months to heal myself." When she reentered the workplace, it was on her own terms.

Pressure-Cooked

In many offices there is an unspoken judgment about who is working hardest and longest, and it creates a culture of competition and guilt.

Stephanie, a buyer for a catalog company, is married with three small daughters. She works hard and smart but finds that in the workforce today, "Time is a measure of how valuable you are to the company. It's not enough to be a solid contributor eight hours a day. Work has to invade your weekends and be all encompassing."

The heat began to rise for Stephanie when she hired a woman who was showing up seven days a week, fifteen hours a day. Not surprisingly, her new hire was quickly promoted to a peer role. "I could see our worlds were going to collide," says Stephanie. "I could not and would not work that way." Stephanie does not see how anyone, including the company, benefits from selling your soul to the company store. She believes it is important to maintain a healthy emotional distance from the company. "They will let you go in a second; it's not a valuable place to invest all of your goods," she says.

Although she hasn't wavered, she still has to suffer the awkwardness of leaving at 5:30 while her peer is still going strong. "I resent having to feel guilty for making it a priority to be home with my family for dinner," she says.

Poached

When is enough, enough? "It's never enough!" says Siobhan, a consulting associate who found that more hours does not mean more productivity.

In her first job out of college, Siobhan wanted to be respected as a real value to the company and quickly fell into the lifestyle of a full-blown workaholic.

She was assigned to a project in which she was relocated to London. It was a change of place, content, and expectations; but what really took her by surprise was that her manager made a personal life one of the priorities for her team. "She told me to make plans and keep them, to get tickets to events and actually go—in other words, no canceling out because of a work crisis." What was most difficult for Siobhan was when her manager told her to just leave the office when the day was over and not take anything home. "Yeah, that was definitely the hardest for me to do," she says.

The team shared joint responsibility, and they all supported each other. This gave Siobhan a sense of balance and clarity. Once she returned to the states, she reverted to her old ways. "This office does not acknowledge a life outside of work," she says. By having seen another way, she resented going back to making choices that constantly put work over her personal life.

One thing she's learned is, "Now I ask directly of the person requesting the work if it is worth my working through the weekend." She's surprised how often the answer is no and thinks of all the times she assumed that the answer would be yes and made the sacrifice.

The irony is she was more productive in London. "The best way I can describe it is: you know those connect-the-dot pictures in children's coloring books? Well, if you hold that picture right up against your face, you have to connect each dot, and even when you are done, you might not see what it is. But if you look at it from some distance, you don't have to waste time actually connecting the dots, you can see it." Time is never a substitute for insightfulness.

Too Hot to Handle

One of the culprits of raising our temperatures at work that really sneaks up on us is boredom. The mundane, old, worn-out routines slowly drain us and our contribution to the company. This happened to Roger, a senior occupation development associate (by the way, don't you love these titles?) for a communications company. Roger loved his job. The projects interested him. The people he worked with were smart and challenged him. He had a great boss and felt recognized and rewarded.

After several years, he sensed something changing. "I no longer looked forward to work anymore," he says. "I was losing interest in what I was doing and found that I had a hard time focusing and completing tasks."

He began looking elsewhere for work, interviewing and talking with all sorts of people. He was feeling that buzz again enjoying the activities of looking for a job. But when he saw these companies up close, he realized that what they had to offer wasn't better than what he currently had. He wondered why he was even thinking of leaving.

He discovered he was simply bored: "I had mastered what had once been challenging, and it had all become too routine." He now has a better understanding of what he needs to keep himself from sinking.

Your Turn

Are you feeling the heat? What are your stories? What kinds of situations do you face each day that are boiling the *real you* out of you one degree at a time?

PART II

Twelve Secrets of Thrivers

I spent a year interviewing people who thrive in the corporate world. They have been in the workplace for a minimum of ten years. They earn a good living, maintain a sense of humor, make genuine relationships, grow as people and professionals, and even get a kick out of it all while keeping perspective. They are from various industries from health care to professional services to biotech. They work in human services, sales, customer service, technology, and support. I learned after spending many hours listening to their stories that they have certain beliefs, attitudes, and clever, sometimes mischievous, ways of keeping their cool while the pot starts to boil. Once I compiled all the information I had collected from over thirty interviews along with what I had been learning from the thousands of employees I had met in my work, twelve practices emerged. Our jobs are how we make our living. We spend at least half our waking hours at work. The Twelve Secrets are a guide to enjoy, grow, and thrive at work.

How You Can Thrive

ONE Be clear how your job serves you to keep cool.

"I grew up in the 1960s, I wanted to improve the world," Jeff, an account executive, laughs. Once he landed a job he had aspired to, director of customer service for a multi-billion-dollar company, a voice nagged at him: "It kept saying, you're missing something, you've lost your torch." He went to a meditation center and reconnected with himself in a deeper and more meaningful way.

"Wow! That really set me on track," he says. "Now, my life's goal, including my job, is to pursue truth."

Paul, a project leader for a professional services firm, places his emphasis on how his job emulates his values in life. "It has to pass what I call the Grandfather's Knee Test," he says, husband and father of two small children.

He values how he will be remembered and how he contributes to the betterment of the lives of others. "When I have my grandchildren on my knee and they ask me what I devoted most of my life to, I want to feel good about my answer."

He realized the importance of the Grandfather's Knee Test when he was offered a job at a condiment company. "You know, ketchup and mustard. The offer was way more money than what I was getting, but it just didn't pass the Grandfather's Knee Test," he says. "Yeah, honey, Gramps produced millions of bottles of ketchup—just think what that means to all those cookouts!" Paul needs his job to feel meaningful in his life.

Jobs serve people in different ways. Gayle, a sales representative for a telephone company and a single woman nearing retirement, is very clear about her life goals and how her job helps reach them.

"I know that having advertising in our Yellow Pages makes a difference in the businesses of my clients—it matters to them. And it matters to me by helping me become the independent old lady I hope to be," she explains. "I used to work for a human services nonprofit company, and it felt like we were just running around chasing our tails. Nothing we did ever felt like it really mattered." Gayle's job gives her a clear predictable way to achieve her goals.

Kathleen, a sales director for a communications company who is married with small children, gives more importance to the benefits, flexibility, and pay than to the meaning of the work.

"My job gives me the finances and flexibility to be the best provider for my children I can be. By giving this purpose top priority, it gives me a feeling of control," she says.

Kathleen's purpose was also put to the test. "Last fall I was offered a promotion for a lot more money, but a lot more travel as well. I turned it down because it meant no more soccer games or visits to the orthodontist during the week. I know flexibility is my priority, and this job gives me that." It's much less important if what she sells has a greater meaning. At this point in her life, she wants to be able to freely attend her children's special activities or be accessible if something comes up.

Stage of life influences the purpose of a job. Carl, a graphic designer, who is recently married and has just taken on a mortgage, says, "At first, I just wanted to learn as much as I could about the different software, but then I got married and we bought a condo. Now the purpose is to financially support my mortgage."

Each one of these folks has given thought to how their job contributes to what they care about most. When their life situation changes, they pay attention to how their job is adapting to their needs. Remembering and being clear about how your job serves you protects you from adapting to anything that is not in your best interest.

Thermostat Adjustment

(Use the Thermostat Adjustment to take a moment to think about how you would answer these questions. This will trigger your awareness of some of the subtle choices you make each day that may be raising your temperature. Awareness is the first step toward reviving your real self.)

It doesn't matter *what* the purpose of your job is. What matters is that you are *conscious* of what it is, paying attention as it changes, and keeping in mind that your job is a choice—*your* choice.

- What is most meaningful to you in your life right now?
- How does your job support that?
- Why did you take this job in the first place? Have your needs changed? How? Does this job meet your new needs? Can it? What changes have to be made?
- Is it time to start advocating for more money, more flexibility, more opportunity to work with particular clients, or learn something new?

TWO Find the right fit. Working in jobs that don't fit is like walking miles in shoes that don't fit. Eventually you can't go any farther.

For Rick, CFO of a biotech firm, a right fit means he has control over his life at work. "It sounds obvious, but it takes a conscious effort to assume control over your job rather than letting it control you," he says. It is easy to get swept up in the daily and weekly crisis—we take our hands off the wheel and let the job drive us. So how do you make sure you are at the wheel?

Rick researches a role he is working toward. He pays close attention not just to the pay, job description, and prestige of a role he's aspiring to, but also to the lifestyle. What hours does that person put in? How much travel does he do? How much flexibility does he have? What kind of people does he interact with?

There's a lot of talk about work/life balance, but often, once we are in a job, many opportunities to negotiate our terms may have been missed. Rick, married, a father of three, a member of his town's school committee, and the bass player for his musical group, the Grateful Dads, knows what he needs for a role to fit and negotiates clear expectations upon taking on a new role.

Once Jeff embraced his purpose of pursuing truth, he discovered that he can't do that every place. He left his job and spent the summer "getting back into my body." Seeing what that job did to him, his wife told him, "Don't go back." After considering many different options, such as doing executive coaching or becoming a middle school teacher or a psychotherapist, he realized what excites him is learning. Now, he enjoys his work with a training firm helping companies provide the best opportunity for their people to grow, learn, and do their best work.

Theresa, a recruiter, found that a right fit for her was to be an individual contributor, a role in which she is given a task to accomplish and is free and independent to accomplish it. She is handed a type of resource to screen for and to come up with four or five ideal candidates. "It's great!" she says. "I just go into my hole, do my thing, and go home. I get a great sense of accomplishment and have an easygoing relationship with everyone who works around me. I really love it." How people work together and set the tone of the office are important aspects of a job being a right fit.

Even when you have a right fit, it can change. Paul had set the expectation that he came in at 10:15 a.m. three mornings a week because he dropped his children off at daycare, and he would not travel more than two days in a row. Paul was challenged to negotiate his schedule when he was invited onto a big, exciting, and highly visible new project with a client he had been working with.

"It was like there was a carrot in exchange for my flesh," he remembers. Management said it was going to require more hours and more travel. "So, at first I asked, does the client like my performance? They said yes, all the data was good there. Then I asked if they had any data on how the client felt about my hours? They said they hadn't asked, but 'thought' the client expected more hours. 'Let's ask,'" he suggested.

He ended up negotiating two mornings instead of three and not traveling more than three days at a time. By having established specific expectations, it gave him a "rudder for the discussion."

"I'm not going to fall into these vague external perceptions about what they *think*," says Paul. "If they do think something I disagree with, if I really can't budge, then I'll suffer the consequences for my choices." It made a difference that he participated in choosing a new schedule rather than having it just assumed he'd adjust.

A right fit doesn't just happen by itself. It needs to be tweaked along the way. Thrivers don't let themselves get boiled unconsciously one degree at a time. When something doesn't feel right, they pay attention and come up with a way to deal with it.

For Gayle, the job was a great fit, but the commute was killing her, even after getting a driving buddy. "We were driving almost two hours each way, longer if the traffic was bad!" she says, sounding exhausted just thinking about it. "The company has several satellite offices around, and I kept putting my name in the hat for a transfer to the office closer to where I live. Finally, something came up. What a difference! I've added eighty hours a month to my life, and I'm not as spent when I get to work or when I get home. It's great!"

She was patient and hopeful that an opportunity would come up. It took a while to get the transfer, but she believed her long commute was temporary and that helped make it more tolerable.

There are so many different options out there. Are you a small-company type, or do you like the huge corporations? Are you a risk taker, or would you prefer more consistency and predictability? Do you like a casual atmosphere, or do you work best with more structure and formality? Are you energized by noise and a busy, chaotic buzz, or does that distract you and you need quiet and solitude? It's easy to see how we can become misfits. We leave getting a right fit to chance unless we are very clear what we need to feel supported and challenged.

"I see people blaming their unhappiness on the work or their boss when I often see they are a poor fit to their job," says Rick. "I had this one kid who wasn't quite cutting it. When I spoke with him about it, he blamed himself, others, and got all demoralized about it. I made some suggestions about other possibilities that might be a better fit for him. Now, he's in the private sector and more successful and much happier."

Once you identify a change you would like to make, see who can help you make that change and talk to them. I had one client who loved her job and the people, but was not happy in Cleveland and desperately wanted to move to Boston. She was lucky to find herself in a networking workshop.

She met a manager from Boston who was looking for someone with her skills. She was so excited. "If I hadn't taken this workshop," she said, "I would never have reached out to anyone in Boston. I'd have been in Cleveland forever." As fate would have it, she landed in a networking workshop, although she helped her luck along by speaking up and asking for what she wanted. We can make our own luck by knowing what we want and asking for it.

Rick sees his peers, managers, and employees as ways to gain information and contacts. He discusses career-track issues with them, asks for information, experiences, networking, guidance, and insights.

"Don't be afraid to talk to people, just learn how." He suggests you frame the discussion around learning and avoid discussing why you are interested in a change. "Don't go to a manager whining and complaining; instead, say, 'I'd like to discuss my career path with you. What options do you see available to me?'"

We just have to muster up the courage. As happy as Theresa is with her job, she found her negotiated four-day workweek was not being observed. "They were scheduling meetings I was expected to attend on my day off," she says. "At first, I was coming in for the meeting and going home. I got up the courage to call in to the meetings." But that was still working on her day off. "Finally, I said if you want me at a meeting, schedule it Monday through Thursday," she said. "They hadn't even realized they were doing that."

Thermostat Adjustment

Your job may be serving its purpose, but it's giving you blisters. What's your size and how does your job fit?

- Is there anything about being at work that *really* bothers you, feels wrong, and no matter what you do, rubs you the wrong way?
- Do others feel the same way?
- Is there a way to bring energy to a solution? For example, one woman I spoke to hated how people swore so much at work, and she found that others were offended by it as well. When she noticed me shrug, she insisted it was really bad. She brought it up with her colleagues with the concern that the language may slip into conversations with clients, which was smart. Instead of just making a case, she made a business case. She suggested they pay for each swear and give the money to the Big Brothers and Sisters organization nearby. The swearing

stopped, and it ended up being a lighthearted "gotcha" joke.

- Who has control over that aspect of the work?
- What is their experience with that behavior or policy?
- Who can help you or introduce you to someone else who can help you?
- What are you doing to contribute to or enable the problem?
- Are there any small things you can do to give yourself more comfort, short term and long term?
- Are there other departments that function more to your liking? Are there opportunities there? Who can give you a better understanding of what it's really like to work there?
- Is it more systemic? Something you just have to learn to live with or go elsewhere? Can you live with it? What is it costing you regarding family, health, and integrity?

THREE Set your thermostat. Consciously setting a limit on how hot and bothered you are willing to get, you protect yourself from boiling over.

Evaluations, client dissatisfaction, mistakes, coming up short on expectations all turn up the temperature. Thrivers set their thermostats. They choose to get only so frustrated. "Screw it! It's a new day tomorrow," says Coleman, a public relations consultant. "Hey, I've been beaten up so many times, so what?" he smirked.

Although he hasn't always been able to say that, "My job would never leave me. I'd wake up at 2 a.m. and drive to the loading dock of the newspaper to see what was written about my client; otherwise, I couldn't sleep." By letting go of that intense attachment to the outcome, he frees himself to have more courage and be more candid.

If we fret too much about losing a customer or disappointing a boss, it paralyzes us and keeps us from putting energy into recovery and solution. Carol, a vice president for human resources, tries to remember, "You can start your day over at any point." When she feels the pressure, she shuts her door and talks herself through it.

"There's always another customer," says Gayle. She believes there are endless opportunities. Rather than get bogged down with a customer who doesn't want to sign on, her *Annie* attitude gives her momentum to get back out there the next day for the next customer, feeding the solution. It has helped her become an unlikely successful sales representative. "When I took my Myers Briggs test, it said I was introverted, so I never even considered sales before."

No one gets through a career without getting bumps and bruises. "I assume the fall is just around the corner. I didn't expect to get where I am," says Paul. "When it happens, though, at least I'll have my integrity and some fun along the way."

Not expecting everything to be perfect, everyone to love everything you do, and receiving applause everywhere you go helps work be a place where, sure, you fall and scratch yourself, but you grow and learn and become a stronger, more experienced, more insightful professional.

"It's not giving up; it's just giving up letting it get to me," says Steve, a partner in a construction company. Accepting that falling is part of the race enables you to take risks, try something new, and stretch outside your comfort zone. This sounds like a cliché, but it's not how many times you fall, it's how long you stay down and what attitude you get up with that makes the difference.

Thermostat Adjustment

Work is emotional. We have a lot invested in our jobs. By having inner resilience, we protect ourselves from the extreme highs and lows and learn from our falls. Over time we bring experience, knowledge, and insight to the marketplace.

- As you remember back to the last time you lost sleep over something you did, or what someone said or didn't say about you, how has your perspective changed since then?
- What does your reaction tell you?
- Are there skills or experiences you can strengthen to be more resilient?
- What is your thermostat set at? Do you let yourself get crazy over things that happen at work? Does your thermostat need adjusting?
- Do you have a mentor who can give you a new perspective? If not, does anyone stand out that might be helpful? What is one gesture you can make this week to initiate a closer relationship with a potential mentor?

FOUR Do the Frog Kick. Finding sheer pleasure in performing your work well and looking for ways to improve gives you freedom and autonomy.

"It's all about the love," says CEO Trammell Crow, one of the top real estate developers in the country. To thrive in your workplace, you need to find something that you love, that excites you, gets you pumped.

"I was in my swim lane this week," smiles Allyson, a marketing manager for an electric company, referring to doing the things she enjoys most about her job. "I don't like everything about my job, but this week I was doing all the parts I love."

"There's always a better way," says Ellen, an administrative assistant at a hospital. She takes pride in what she does and likes the feeling of doing a good job. When she saw the shape of the bookkeeping paperwork at her job, she put her head down, organized it, and made it more efficient. "I got it down to a system anyone could pick up and work with," she says smiling.

Michele, a recruiter for nurses, loves what she does. "Although, it wouldn't matter what it was, I just love the feeling of doing a job well," she says.

"I like doing what I learn in trainings; it works!" says Gayle. (I know what you're thinking. I promise I did not set her up to say that!) Gayle sees results by applying what she has learned, and she just gets a kick out it. Learning is enjoyable. It gives confidence and understanding. There are many venues for learning and growing within an organization and outside of it.

I've learned there are three types of participants in trainings: the Vacationers, who think since they don't have to answer the phones they can take a cruise; the Prisoners, whose managers told them to take the program because they need it and are ticked off and determined to make everyone else miserable; and the Learners, who genuinely look at the day as a way to meet people, learn something, be reminded of something, think in a new way, and gain some real value. Which one are you when you go to trainings?

Henry is a participant I had in a training for a chemical company. The program was designed around a 360-degree feedback report, which is a compilation of data from people who work all around him. Before the program I was not sure how to handle Henry for three days because his report was all positive gaps, meaning he was exceeding expectations in all categories.

At the end of the three days he came up to me and said, "Sharon, this was so hard!" When I asked him why, his face scrunched up and he squinted his eyes and said, "Just muscles I'm not used to using!" Even with all that positive feedback, he was invigorated by learning new things. Thrivers find a way to get a kick out of their work life because they stay open to newness in familiar experiences.

Enjoying a job ebbs and flows. Thrivers pay attention to how they feel about their work. When Roger discovered he was bored with the job he had once loved, he contacted the legal department of his company. He had been interested in what they do and at one point in time had considered law school. He asked them if they had any openings, but none were available. "I started volunteering to help in any way I could with their projects just to get to know them and for them to get to know me," he said. He also started taking law courses at the local university.

"I ended up getting offered a job in that department, and I love it!" he says. "But it took a year and a half." What really surprised him was this: "Once I started working toward a new role, that was all I needed to feel challenged and re-engaged, I started enjoying my regular job more again, too!" The more alive we are and engaged in our work, the higher our performance and the stronger our position is to negotiate what we need to stay feeling alive; it's a cycle.

Paul's definition of success is that work is a "place to learn, grow, meet people, deepen my truth to myself, and help others." How we define success can free us up to grow in our jobs or limit us. Paul looks for "where the passion and energy is." He seeks an organic meaning to the workplace, and every week "picks something scary and dives in." By choosing self-development as his main goal, Paul is free to be in the moment, fully experiencing the ups and downs. It gives him a healthy detachment when things are either going very well or not well at all.

Someone once made the mistake of telling Cheryl, a finance advisor for an investment firm, that she'll never make it in the finance business because she's a woman. Now she just loves proving them wrong. "I am fanatical about bringing in the business. I make a lot of money and that gives me freedom," she says.

Kathleen values the autonomy that comes with doing her job well. "I'm getting my work done, everybody's managed, and I handle everything I need to handle. If I want to go to my son's soccer game in the afternoon, I go," she says. "No questions asked." But, she warns, "It's not enough to be good, you have to *know* you're good."

In ideal situations people give recognition and rewards to those who bring value, but oftentimes, people are so busy, it gets overlooked. How do you know if you're good? Look objectively at your data. Are people seeking you out to be involved in projects? Do people choose you to handle something when it's important? Do you contribute in some way to bringing in new business, repeat business?

Thermostat Adjustment

Of course we can't always be wide-eyed doing the frog kick everyday, but how we choose to look at situations, people, and our jobs can make a difference in our level of sheer enjoyment of working. I found Thrivers choose to look at things through a lens that energizes and inspires them.

- When you listen to yourself describe situations and people at work, what words and phrases do you most often use? What is your tone of voice saying?
- What would happen if you try playing with new words and begin describing things in new ways?
- What first attracted you to your job? Where do you get most enjoyment in your workday? (And you can't pick when you go home!) How can you bring more of that into your work experience?
- What interests you most about your industry? Are there opportunities to learn more about that? What's the next challenge for you? What could you be doing to get the juices flowing in that area?
- What manageable improvement in your workplace can you make your own and put your stamp on?

FIVE Make Real-ationships. Making authentic relationships and having a friend or two at work that you can trust and laugh with is cool.

I meet thousands of corporate employees a year. People moan and groan to me about management, staff, and clients, and then I ask them what they love most about their job and they break into a big grin and exclaim, "The people!" Go figure. The people we work with are the heaven *and* the hell of our experiences at work. Thrivers don't love everybody, yet they are authentic in their relationships at work and have a friend they can trust.

Steve was happy for Jim, but disappointed for himself, because Jim was leaving the company for a new opportunity. "Jim gets me laughing about things and helps me through the tough times," he smiles. "I'm going to miss him." The workweek is very dynamic and emotional. It helps to have someone who really gets you, you get him or her, they see the insanity the same way you do and can make you laugh about it.

"We've been through a lot together, two mergers, all kinds of changes in leadership, policies, and expectations. Most of us have been together for between ten or fifteen years," says Kathleen. "We take care of each other." Although most people have several jobs throughout their careers, sometimes a core group of people stick it out with one company and develop a real history together.

Like any long-term relationship, that bond does not happen quickly or magically. It is built over time through experiences both good and bad. The genuineness of our relationships at work determines how boiled we get. Thrivers benefit from making *real-ationships* at work. Jeff puts his value of truth into action and finds that people respond—family, friends, and people at work.

"I like to swap ideas, get to know people, learn through people, and just have fun!" says Paul. Sustaining genuineness can be tricky. One thing Paul has noticed he needs to do is monitor himself for phoniness for the sake of success. "I can hear the change in my voice. I can hear myself laughing along with the upper management's joke, engaging in the chitchat, trying to paint this picture of my life as being this interesting thing, the restaurants, vacations. Every time I hear myself using the word 'wonderful,' I automatically know I'm off," he confesses.

It takes courage for Paul to admit this. As we lose genuineness one degree at a time, we increase the temperature and are boiling before we know it. Has a friend or spouse ever commented on your "work self"? Paul makes it a priority to foster *real-ationships*. There is a fuzzy line between genuine relationships and purposefully building targeted relationships for the sake of climbing the corporate ladder.

This is not to say that it is categorically brown-nosing to build relationships with leadership, but if you are sacrificing your real self for that relationship, it can raise your temperature. Peter, a manager for a top four accounting firm, says he considers his workplace the same as his neighborhood, "Even though this is a big firm, it is still comprised of people. I'd talk about baseball with a neighbor; why would it be any different with a partner or my staff?"

It sounds simple enough, but situations crop up that catch us by surprise and challenge us. Paul found himself on a slippery slope when he was asked to lead a strategy session on a post-acquisition; the issue of discussion was establishing trust (how apropos). A huge number of people showed up. A lot of stuff had happened that eroded trust with the new regime. Some of it was misunderstanding, some misleading. The consensus from the group was deep mistrust of the new CEO.

"The choice is what do I report to the CEO, who is on the record as not wanting to hear the bad stuff. Do I tell her 'a lot of people don't trust you,' or do I paint a not-so-bad picture with words?" he questioned.

Paul was challenged to put his beliefs into action. "I knew I would feel small, like a wimp if I didn't listen to my heart and tell the truth." By having the courage to be true to his self and reporting the truth to the CEO, he gave her the opportunity to face and deal with some important issues that were drawing energy from the company. No, he didn't get fired. He made a friend. The CEO grew to consider Paul someone she could trust. When we take the risk to honestly open up to others, we give them a way to open up to us.

Thermostat Adjustment

It takes prioritizing authenticity, courage to be your real self, and having someone you can share honestly with and laugh with at work to protect you from the heat.

- Are you phony? How do you describe the line between being your real self and being professional? How much of your true self gets lost in translation?
- How does your tone of voice change when you are talking to management? Why? What does that tell you?
- Are there ways for you to more honestly express yourself at work without sacrificing credibility?
- Do you have a true buddy at work? If not, is there anyone you can trust and would be fun to get to know better? What quick and easy thing can you do to initiate more interaction with him or her?

me, I can support myself until I am ready to do something else," she says.

The side business gives her more confidence when negotiating different expectations the company has of her. For example, she remembers a surprise when checking into a hotel for a training: "I arrived the night before and the hotel clerk said, 'Your roommate is expecting you.' I was like, my what? The company expected me to slip into a hotel room with a stranger without ever having told me? I asked the desk clerk for my own room and would settle it later."

She called her manager the next morning. "I didn't start out with it, but I made it clear that I had my own room for the week and would be expensing it in full," she says. "He was fine with it." Her spirit of independence gives her the courage to not settle but to speak up and negotiate terms that she and the company can live with. Unconsciously settling is boiling.

Building a strong network of associates and friends in the business multiplies our alternatives. I was visiting the Fish Show in Boston with my friend Patty. She's a broker in the business. I felt as if I was with one of the Who's Who of the fish industry. It wasn't just that she knew so many people, it was how people sought her out, were so happy to see her, and respected her. When things took a turn for the worse in her job, the phone was ringing off the hook with competitive offers.

Flexibility in the marketplace builds confidence and independence. It can be something as simple as keeping a resume updated that can keep us agile. The daunting task of updating a resume can become a big threshold in our minds that influences us to adapt to circumstances that raise the temperature.

Living paycheck to paycheck and being overly dependent on our jobs limits our freedom, spontaneity, creativity, and ultimately, our value to the company creating a spiral that curls in on itself. The key to an effective lily pad is that it is independent of the company. If your lily pad is that you have options in your company, or a retirement plan, as good as that is, it is a vulnerable backup plan as we have seen in cases where the company did not make good on its promises.

Thermostat Adjustment

A zillion things get in the way of saving, wisely investing, and building a nest egg; but without alternatives, we're cooked.

- If your job fell apart today, how long would you be able to support yourself without working? Do you have other viable alternatives?
- Are your expenses absorbing most of your income? What quick and easy adjustments can you make on your lifestyle to live more frugally?
- How much money can you afford to put away in a special not-to-be-touched account per week?

- How would your experience of your job change if you had more money saved?
- What are the two or three critical obstacles to your saving account? How can you overcome one of those obstacles?
- Do any of your friends or family have a financial consultant they trust? Would you consider meeting with a financial consultant to discuss more variety in your financial situation?
- How can you deepen and expand your quantity and quality of relationships in your industry?
- When did you last update your resume?

SEVEN: Have a toad-le blast! Enjoying a joke, having fun, and even getting a little mischievous once in a while makes work life worthwhile.

Dick Eaton, CEO (Chief Energizing Officer) of Leapfrog Innovations, believes, "A company that laughs, lasts." One sure way to know when you and your colleagues are in a boiling pot is when nobody can take a joke. Everyone is going through the motions of being oh so serious. Is there such a thing as too much professionalism? If you feel you are the only one who sees the "seriousness," you might be the office downer and could stand to lighten up! Try seeing the movie *Office Space* or watching the TV series *The Office*—they're funny.

"Oh, I have to say, we have fun around here," says Kathleen. "We work with so many types of people—the Hydrolox guy [vendor], lawyers, and people from the medical clinic. People are just so funny! The other day this guy was in here telling us about how his wife likes it when he gains weight because that way she doesn't have to worry about other girls looking at him. That just cracked us up! I was still laughing in the car on my way home."

Thrivers giggle as they tell their stories, and I'm thinking, "I guess you had to be there." Jay, a manager for a telephone company, was telling me about a guy he works with who is deathly afraid of dogs. "We sent him on a call, and doesn't he get bit by a dog," he laughs. "So, in the next meeting

I told him the client was suing him for damages to his dog."

I thought the story was funny, but Jay thought it was *really* funny. It occurred to me it was because he knows the guy, can picture him, and was able to see the bigger humor of it. "But," Jay warns, "You gotta know who can take it and who can't; otherwise, it's just mean." There is an important distinction between seeing the humor in people and making fun of them.

Bureaucracy produces stupidity, and if somebody doesn't acknowledge it, we all go crazy. Joan, a director of nursing at a psychiatric hospital, sees the insanity in some of the policies. "Sometimes they are so ridiculous, we write other policies that make the first ones impossible to abide by," she says with a wry smile, "Each day I get up wondering which rules I need to break in order to not break the rules."

Companies don't always make it easy to be a Thriver. Kathleen's company was withholding the compensation checks she depended on to pay her bills. They gave her a song and dance about why, but she believed they were holding onto them to maximize the interest. She found a harmless, yet little mischievous way to even the score.

"I go home in the middle of the day each week and clean my house," she says. "Then I go back to work." When she saw the puzzled look on my face, she explained, "It makes a big difference when I get home that night to have to a clean house! It's like I have a cleaning service." Someone could argue this may not exactly be ethical, but to Kathleen, it gives her a sense of control and that sustains her sense of self.

Cheryl has a work hard/play hard ethic, but she confesses she's not afraid to "make a fool" of herself. She approaches her work with a playful attitude and is quick to laugh at herself when she makes a mistake or doesn't know something.

Being irreverent comes with its risks. Ask Carl, who paid a price with his manager for his sense of humor.

"Because I got my work done quickly, I would work on my own little projects. For example, I took a picture of a bald eagle soaring the heights and compiled the Energizer Bunny hanging in its jowls and put it up on my cubicle. A lot of my colleagues thought it was hysterical, and people were asking for copies of it," he explains. "But my manager told me to take it down because it was disrespectful to a branded product and that if I had time for that, she'll double my load." Come on, disrespect for a branded product? It's not a person, for heaven's sake!"

Carl was most disappointed that his manager did not see that his playful projects were ways he was becoming more proficient in different types of software, which he incorporated into his work by making more impressive documents. "It was just lighthearted fun," he says. "I notice the one that is quickest to get offended sets the standard for what is offensive."

Humor has its obvious benefits and risks. What a shame it would be if Carl squelched his funny spirit just because his manager couldn't take a joke (see practice number nine on how to handle office jerks).

Everybody loves music! Rick delivered the highlights of his financial report at the annual stockholders' meeting to the tune of "Do You Like Pina Coladas?" Cathy, a public relations coordinator for the company's stop smoking campaign, wrote some parody songs for the holiday party ("If you don't stop smoking … Fa la la la la … You'll be choking"). Both of them received a great response. "Now they expect me to write songs for every occasion. It really contributes to camaraderie in the office," says Cathy.

The work environment sheds light on a small fraction of who we really are. In my training programs we do an icebreaker that asks participants to share one "little known fact" about themselves. The beauty of the exercise is that we see each other in a fuller way. I've had night scuba divers, contestants on game shows, and college sports stars. The list goes on and on. You can feel the change in the room when someone goes from introducing himself or herself as the technical support associate to a "Sudoku expert." Thrivers find a way to bring their humanity into the workplace.

Thermostat Adjustment

Thrivers find ways to bring their real selves to the office. Without a spirit of fun and humor, who are we?

- Anything funny happen today?
- What comical team does your work team remind you of? *The Office*? *Saturday Night Live*? *South Park*? *Reno 911*?
- What or who suffocates humor in your office? Why? What causes that?
- Do *you* take things too seriously? What price do you pay for that?
- How would morale, productivity, and creativity benefit if there was a lighter mood?
- What are some dangers of joking around?
- What are some harmless ways you can bring a little humanity and fun into your workday?

EIGHT Chill once in a while. Whether it's five minutes or five weeks, knowing you need a break keeps you refreshed.

Composers and choreographers know audiences need a break, and a break is change. The pressures of doing business can make us forget our basic needs—never mind emotional needs! How many times have you forgotten to eat or go to the bathroom? We were discussing this in one of my programs, and a participant said she was jealous of smokers. I asked why and she said, "Because they get to leave their desks and go outside for a few minutes three or four times a day."

I thought, how sad. But she was right. Do the rest of us give ourselves a chance to just step away from our desks to enjoy a few minutes of fresh air? Management probably worries that people take too many breaks. There is a difference between a brief change of scenery and instant messaging with colleagues all day.

A break doesn't have to mean not working; it can mean working in a new way. Change is a break. It can be as simple as adding a tiny moment of delight to your day by doing any of these activities:

- Rearranging your cubicle, updating your pictures of family and friends, adding a back support for your chair
- Taking a different route to work or to the restroom

- Taking/not taking public transportation one day a week
- Putting some cilantro in your packed lunch
- Having lunch at an out-of-the-way little bistro
- Inviting someone new to join you for lunch
- Wearing something a little different for you, a different color pair of socks, type of shoes, tie, jewelry, anything
- Getting a new haircut, a nose ring ... (I'm kidding, I think)

Thrivers seek out little changes to the daily routine. They keep new places, faces, vistas, and images flowing in and out of their daily life. "I always took the most direct route to work," says Steve. "Now, occasionally I take some back roads. It's fun. I see people out and about in their morning routines of walking the dog, the kids boarding the bus." He starts his day with a new view.

"I sat and finished my coffee with my wife this morning," says Allen, an auto claims representative, "and it really made a difference."

When Donna, a receptionist, was replacing her family photos, she laughed, "The pictures of my family that I've had on my desk are so old, my husband has hair in them."

Jill flies a lot for her job. "I like meeting people on the plane," she says. One of her best friends she calls Joe Plane because she met him on the plane. We each have our own ways of bringing a fresh outlook to our jobs. Inspired by Jill, the next time I was on a plane I very uncharacteristically started chatting with the gentleman next to me. It was lovely until I spilled a full glass of red wine all over his very expensive white shirt.

It's more comfortable for me to push myself to go see something outside the conference center. Recently, I was in Austin, Texas, and went to watch the bats fly out from under the bridge where they live to get their nightly meal. There were thousands of them. It takes a real effort for me to do that. It's so much easier to just head back to my room and order room service, which I do too. I'm always glad I've made the effort to go on a little field trip and glad when I've decided to just chill.

Have you heard people brag about not taking vacation? And you're thinking, yeah, and you're making *us* need it more! Steve has no problem taking vacation. Although, there is a time to take time off and a time not to. "If we are a few weeks from getting our certificate of occupancy, it's not a good time to take a vacation," he says. Your company offers you time off, it's no one else's fault if you don't find a way to take it.

Thrivers know they have complex and changing needs and find creative ways to satisfy them. Feeling bored, Rick took advantage of his company's international exchange program by applying for a transfer to his wife's homeland, Denmark. They lived there for two years. "That was a real mental breather for me, even though the work was the same. It felt so good to be doing it in such a new environment."

"I was struggling with issues of balance and spirituality in my life. I wanted more than just a career," says Tom, CFO of a local newspaper. He told his story in an article in the *Boston Globe,* August 5, 2001. He went on a Tuscan Sabbatical, which is a weeklong retreat in Florence, Italy, for entrepreneurs and executives who need time to reflect on the direction and status of their professional and personal lives. Joseph D'Arrigo, the creator of the Tuscan Sabbatical says in the article, "I founded the program after a six-year period of logging in sixteen-hour days. I found time for family during weekends and holidays, but something was always missing."

Reflection is how we discover insights into how things are related and interconnected; we gain perspective, we deepen our understanding of situations and people, and we expand our thinking. In the hectic pace of most companies, time to reflect is neglected.

Thomas, a patent attorney and litigator at a corporate law firm, spends a month in silence at a meditation retreat in rural India. "The transition can be difficult. You're coming out of a high-speed, high-energy, hard-driving world, and you're moving to a much quieter, more peaceful place," he says. He has done this every year since 1980. Thrivers give priority to having time to get out of the noise of the day-to-day to think and digest what is going on around them.

Not all of us can afford to go to India or Italy. But a break can be adding something new. David, a manager of a design firm, likes having more than one job. "Besides extra income, having more than one job gives me other rewards. Teaching architecture at a local college a few times a week adds some variety to my otherwise routine office job. Freelance writing gives me a chance to research and learn new things that I don't get to know in my other jobs; it keeps my brain oiled," he says.

It can but doesn't have to be a job. It could be volunteering with a youth group, taking a dance class. Jeff takes hip-hop classes on Saturday mornings. "I love to dance!" he says. "It doesn't advance my career, and I'm married so I'm not doing it to meet women, although I wish I'd thought of it when I was younger. It fulfills me!"

I just received an e-mail about a colleague who has been doing improvisational theater in Chicago as a hobby. The e-mail was announcing that she has just taken a job with a company that uses improvisation as a learning tool in corporations. Sometimes a break or change can actually take us to a new opportunity.

Thermostat Adjustment

There is only one CEO (Chief Energizing Officer) of your life and that is you. You are not any good to you, the company, your customers, or your family and friends if you become boiled. Recognize when you need a few minutes of fresh air, new music on your iPod, or a getaway and find a way to provide it.

- What times of the day or situations do you typically need rejuvenation? What can you plan or prepare for those moments to give you a breather?
- What physical changes to your space (or to you) will stimulate a new perspective?
- What do you typically do with your time off? How do you feel when you return? What would help you return from time off most refreshed and rejuvenated?
- Are there any opportunities in your community that would bring new faces and places into your routine? Local government? Adult education as a teacher or student? A choir or band? Yoga instead of pilates?
- What is one thing you can do this month that would take you off your beaten path?
- How can you routinely change your routine?

NINE Handle the office jerks. Knowing that every office has one helps.

Most people fall under the bell curve. There are a few who are just fun to work with; you love them, they love you, it's heavenly. Then there are the few who seem to set their alarm in the morning to get up and make everyone miserable. Hopefully, for you, that's just a very few and that you're not married to one. The rest of us fall somewhere in between with our good days and not so good days, and most days are somewhere in between.

Unfortunately, there is no magic wand to make the office jerk into an angel. Thrivers found them to be a drain as well. "We call her 'The Beast,'" says Debi, a mutual bond manager. "I just limit face-to-face time with her the best I can. I communicate with her through e-mail or phone mail and leave stuff on her chair when she's out of her office." Avoidance is a good strategy, but not always possible.

I had been delivering a customer service program to all the employees of a finance company. I quickly learned about Oscar (seriously, that was his name), a client whom everyone complained about. He was rude, abusive, demanding, arrogant, entitled, and everyone hated him. He was also a huge source of revenue so he wasn't going anywhere soon. I began referring to Oscar as if I knew him, when every once in a while someone would smile and say, "I don't have a problem with Oscar, his bark is louder than his bite." Some people were able to not take him seriously, not take his comments personally, and work with him.

Kathleen is amused by her office jerk. "I look at him as if he were a character in a movie. Sometimes it can be very funny how he behaves, geez!"

Paul makes a point to observe as well; he looks for the unmet human need. "We were at this client meeting strategizing the next implementation. Well, she shows up for what reason I'm not sure. No one had invited her and we didn't feel a need for her. Anyway, that's fine until we get to who is going to do the delivery, and she barges in saying she is the best candidate and why aren't we considering her. The client doesn't know she is way overbooked as it is."

Paul's first reaction was to get angry with her. "I wanted to scream at her. She barges into a meeting she's not invited to and now is setting expectations she can't deliver on. Why? When I wondered, what is the unmet human need here, it occurred to me that she has a need to be recognized and included. So I acknowledged her knowledge and experience and suggested she play the role of consultant to our team rather than be the day-to-day delivery person. That was very well received. I felt I understood her better and had a stronger approach to our implementation than if she had not shown up." It can be very gratifying to discover the person under the monster suit.

I had an office jerk come into my program once. Being very green as a training facilitator, I was into the first morning of a three-day training on consultative skills when the door flung open and in came the emotional equivalent of Pig Pen from the Peanuts cartoon. He was definitely a Prisoner (someone who really doesn't want to be in a training session but is forced to attend by his employers). He was here to make everyone miserable. I ignored him hoping a cup of coffee and a bagel would get him over it.

When I got to him for introductions, he said, "My name is Joe, and my objective is to get the hell out of here!" Weak knees and palms sweating, I smiled and kept going. By 10 a.m. we were all going down the black hole. (Did I mention this was a *three-day* program?)

I was either going to start crying and run out of the room or strangle Joe, but instead I decided to go to my last resort, the content I was delivering. "Hey, Joe, you really don't seem happy to be here, wanna tell me about it?" I surrendered.

"They want us to give great client service when they just cut the staff in half and took away our overtime," he burst out. It turned out everyone else was being polite, but these folks were beaten down and had nothing left for role-plays on "asking questions" and "confirming understanding."

We talked about it for forty-five minutes and got to what I now call the inhale/exhale. "So, what do you guys want to do? We're here for three days, anyone have cards, wanna play poker?" I asked.

"Well, these are good skills in case we go somewhere else," someone piped up. (Oh, great, everyone quits after my program, but I don't care; I'm just trying to survive.)

End of story: we had a great three days together fully exploring and practicing the art of consultative skills. Joe taught me that sometimes what we find under the office jerk suit is just one of us in a difficult situation. It turned out Joe was cool.

What if the office jerk is your boss? That is definitely more difficult. Michele worked for a woman who, depending on her mood, was unpredictable as to whether your head was on the chopping block or not. "I learned to let it roll off and walk away," she says. Her deep desire to do a good job fueled her to overcome the nasty disposition of her boss and just put her head down and do what she thought was best. Although, "Sometimes I had to go to the powers-that-be over her," she says. "I would not let her negativity make me leave something I love."

Peter was a business analyst for a technology department of a university when he worked for someone who frowned upon his ambition and his taking initiative. When there was a meeting coming up that he felt he could contribute to and would be helpful to him, he asked to attend, as long as it was appropriate. His boss's reaction still surprises him,

"She told me to stop worrying about other people's calendars." He realized then and there it wasn't going to work out.

I asked him what he thought prompted her to react that way. "She saw me as a big shot from a fancy firm, like I was showboating," Peter says. As we continued to discuss what it must have been like to be her, we both began to see she may have been afraid for her position. The first reaction might be to leave and get another job and, for Peter, that has proven to be the best response, but sometimes the devil you know is better than the one you don't.

When Kathleen worked for a jerk, she saw her as a character in a book or movie. That gave Kathleen some distance so as not to take her boss personally. She kept her eye out for a transfer, but in the meantime, "I confronted her when I had to. I'm not going to be a doormat for anyone."

Rick was surprised when a partner he found difficult to work with turned out to sing his praises to those who were inquiring about hiring him. He believes that made the difference to getting offered a job he is very happy in now.

Working for an office jerk is much more challenging than working with one. If there is any way to uncover the person under the monster suit, that boss could end up being your greatest advocate.

Thermostat Adjustment

No doubt about it, office jerks can get our blood boiling. And it's not you; office jerks are difficult, but it can be incredibly satisfying to find the human being under the monster suit or to find a way to be insulated from their wrath.

- What physical reactions do you have to your office jerk?
- How do you typically respond to him or her?
- Like Dr. Phil says, "How's that working for you?"
- As you observe yourself, what do your reactions say about you?
- Is there anyone else who seems to have an easier time with the office jerk? How does the office jerk respond differently to him or her?
- Are you afraid of your office jerk in any way? What are you afraid of?
- What do you think it must be like to be him or her? What is that person's unmet human need?
- Would you know if you were the office jerk, difficult boss, or impossible client? How would you know? What price might you be unknowingly paying?

TEN Hey, shit happens. Pardon my French, but sometimes it's unavoidable.

There is no perfect world. Setting your thermostat can help minimize the price to pay, but we are human beings. Cubicle life is a place of moving parts. There are so many things that can and do go wrong: missed deadlines, lost revenue, unclear expectations. If you don't have some way to protect yourself, it can really drive anyone nuts!

"I just yell out loud, 'Oh f---!' and people start laughing and we get over it. I know last week's crisis is this week's joke," says Theresa. "Other times, I just suck it up and move on, period."

Coleman focuses on "what *can* be done to recover. Who cares how it got this way, how are we going to get back on track?"

Problems at work can work their way into our psyches, which can be a way to be creative. "I wrestle with it till I get closure I can live with," says Michele. She systematically looks at the issue from many different angles until she comes up with a solution that is good for the client, the company, and her. Like a dog with a bone, she enjoys the challenge and process of resolving the crisis. By being detached from worrying about who screwed up, she is more focused on the uncharted answer.

Sometimes the harder we work the more things get screwed up. That's when Paul gets a little Zen: "Turn to water, and flow around the obstacles."

Rick figures there is always a way out: "I don't take deadlines seriously. I'll call a client who is expecting three data assessment reports by Tuesday and ask if they are going to need all of them. Inevitably, they aren't going to get to all of them till the end of the week, so I buy myself and my staff a few days to breathe."

My staff from what became known as "The Project from Hell" wishes I had known what Rick knows. My project was a disaster because I did such a poor job managing the expectations and demands of a tough client. Everyone had to run around like chickens with their heads cut off, putting in insane hours trying please the client. Rick gives himself and those around him breathing space by having the courage and negotiation skills to keep deadlines fluid.

Whatever you do, don't simmer! It causes heart attacks. Debi has learned to express herself in a way that invites collaboration. "I *want* to say, 'You stupid idiots, why are you putting out marketing materials with all wrong information instead of consulting my department first?' But what I do say is, 'I notice the marketing materials have required supplements and correction memos. I'm thinking it may be because you aren't getting the information you need when you need it. Can we talk about a way for you to get what you need when you need it?' What is really profound is that it settles me down and helps me feel more collaborative, too."

Thrivers seek ways to express themselves without judging, blaming, or avoiding. Mary Helen Gillespie, The Savvy Manager, suggests in her *Boston Globe* column, Beyond Blame, to substitute the three words, "Who screwed up?" with "So, what's next?"

"Uncertainty is what I have the most difficulty with," says Peter. It's not that things are going wrong that is most stressful, it's the fear of having nothing to do when he comes to work. Paul has to sell himself onto projects and actively keep his dance card full. Even with the best-laid plans, things change. "I had client work for at least eight months out, and all of a sudden the client decided to go in-house for the work, and I was left hanging," he remembers. He gets a sense of control by keeping proactive, seeking out partners and colleagues and inquiring what they are involved with and asking what is coming up in the pipeline.

"I don't like it when people ask me what they can do to help, so I don't do that to others," he says. He finds it's much more valuable to come up with ideas how he might be helpful or add value. Peter finds lunch is a good venue, "I share with them where I see myself, ask them how that might be valuable in their projects, who else should I be talking to." He finds that these conversations remind decision makers of who he is and that he's available, as well as provide a great exchange of helpful information. By regularly taking initiative, he manages the anxiety of uncertainty.

Thermostat Adjustment

Being a perfectionist is a killer. It helps to face that things are going to go wrong, people (maybe even you) are going to make mistakes—sometimes really stupid mistakes—and there will be damage. Knowing this frees us to think strategically and have our own way to respond that cultivates growing and learning.

- Do you believe things should go right so they will?
- Do you believe that because you do things a certain way, everyone should?
- What makes you believe that?
- Do you assume that because someone makes a stupid mistake they are stupid?
- When you think of times you have made mistakes, where was the breakdown in the process?
- What do you think is most important for things to go right? How do you ensure those keys are in place in your day-to-day interactions?
- What do you need most from others when something has gone wrong? Management? Staff? Colleagues? Clients? How do you express what you need? Do you provide that for others?

- What do you focus on first when something goes wrong? How effective is that? What might be a more effective sequence of things to focus on?

ELEVEN Be grateful and show it.

"Whatever you may feel about your job, the company you work for, your boss, or your co-workers, your job supports you, feeds you, helps you, and gives you opportunities to keep growing and finding fresh opportunities," says Lewis Richmond, author of *Work as a Spiritual Practice.*

Gratitude is only valuable when it is real. You can't just put on a Pollyanna face and be thankful for your job. It doesn't work that way. Thrivers think about and acknowledge what they appreciate about their jobs.

Coleman is grateful for the tangible recognition he gets from his work: "Promotions, big contracts, a mention in the newsletter," he says. "Nobody gives me a promotion for coaching Little League."

After working for nonprofits and jobs where things were very ambiguous, Gayle appreciates the objectivity of her job: "Either you make your numbers or you don't. The rewards are distributed directly to performance." She likes that feeling of knowing exactly where she stands. Having a sense of gratitude for your job gives you a positive outlook that lifts you and those around you.

It is very seductive to get caught up in the complaining about the office. "I know the deal and my choice is to stay," says Kathleen. "It'd be wrong for me to blame and feel sorry for myself. I get five weeks vacation, a good salary, I like the people

I work with, the freedom, and the variety of my customers."

"I'm glad that I like getting up in the morning and going to work," says Ellen because she knows what it's like to dread going to work. She works in a hospital with the nursing staff and enjoys being around them. "I catch the fever," she says, meaning the fever of caring for others.

Michele feels lucky to work for her company, "The owners bring integrity to everything they do, and they are human to deal with." No job is perfect and every job has something to appreciate. Thrivers do not lose sight of how their job benefits their life.

Thrivers distinguish themselves by being grateful for how people support them and find genuine ways to express their appreciation. "Nobody says 'thank you' anymore," observes Debi. She's right.

I was delivering a customer service program to all the employees of a company and then going back to deliver a managing customer service program. One woman came up to me after one of the first sessions and asked if I was going to be working with the managers. When I said yes, she asked, "Would you tell them something for me? Would you tell them it makes a big difference when someone says 'thank you.'"

Joan tries to send a handwritten note to someone on her staff that has stepped up beyond expectations. One of her staff came to work with an overnight bag just in case she had to stay the extra shift. Joan sent her a note, and when the woman received it, she couldn't believe it, she was so appreciative. "It really meant a lot," she said.

Last year Michele won a prestigious award that was chosen by a companywide vote. As flattered as she was, she knew she couldn't do it herself. "There's no 'I' in team," she says. We've all heard it till it's almost funny, but Michele really lives it. When I asked her how she expresses her appreciation for the support she gets, she said, "I say 'thank you.' It's as simple as that."

We each need to find our own personal way of showing appreciation. It doesn't have to be complicated or a lot of work, although it does need to be real. Think about the last time someone expressed gratitude to you for something you did and how that made you feel.

Thermostat Adjustment

- What are three things about your job that you are really grateful for?
- How would someone else know you appreciate your job? What would they hear you say or see you do *or* not hear you say or not see you do?
- What would you miss most about your job?
- Who are you thankful for? Do they know you appreciate them? This doesn't mean saying, "Thank you for shopping at Wal-Mart." How can you show your appreciation in a meaningful way?

TWELVE: Perform a balancing act. Keeping it all in perspective is a must.

Soccer games, conference calls, client meetings, spouse's birthday, mother's biopsy, new employee starting, friend going through a divorce, dinner party Saturday night, status report due, big presentation on Tuesday, doctor's appointment, colleague getting recognized for your work, snowstorm, in-laws coming for the weekend, Ahh! How can anyone possibly have work/life balance? It's impossible *all* the time.

The first chairwoman of the board for a *Fortune* 500 company I was working with was speaking at a conference. She was speaking in front of seven hundred new senior managers and opened the floor for questions. A woman stepped up to the microphone and asked how she keeps a work/life balance given she lives in California and works in New York City.

"Well," she stumbled, "I don't have children, but I do have two very demanding dogs." She laughed while no one else did. "And I make sure I am home for Friday date night with my husband." I'm not going to speculate on the quality of that date, but I know what it would be if it were with me, sharing leftover spaghetti watching *Dateline* and zonked out by 9:30.

Joan has some creative ways to strike that balance, particularly in how she uses her allotted time off. "It's about feeding the soul," she says. "I take a day off the week after Thanksgiving to decorate my house for the holidays, and that feeds me for the whole month." Vacation time doesn't necessarily have to be a trip or renting a cottage for two weeks. Joan takes another day off in early spring to put away winter clothes, get the home ready for summer with bathing suits, towels, the yard pool, and put the *Flying Scott* (a racing sailboat) in the water.

Another myth Joan blows apart is to separate job and home. "I find bringing the kids to work and having them have a picture of the working 'me' and introducing my colleagues to my home life rounds me out for both them and me."

When Steve's daughter began working for him, he was surprised how his relationship with her deepened. He also noticed people began to see him differently, and his image at work improved. Often times we have the best of both worlds, why not let them complement each other and look for ways to bring them together? Otherwise, the work world can be in conflict with the home world.

When George, an investments manager for an insurance company, brought his three boys in, one of his colleagues said about his youngest, "He's the Xerox reduction of George!" A moment they all enjoyed.

There is no magic wand to balancing work and home, but what does help is being aware of what your soul is hungry for and creative in feeding it. If you love the Wimbledon, schedule a half day to come home early and have a vodka tonic watching Federer and Roddick hammer it out.

Thrivers may not have constant balance, but they do have a perspective of the place their job occupies in their life.

- "My job is a part of my life, not my whole life," says Theresa.
- "At the end of the day, it's just a job, it does not make me *me*," says Carol, an HR associate.
- "My priorities are the four Fs: Family, Fun, Fitness, and Finances," says Kathleen, "in that order."
- "The key for me is not to just have a life outside work, but to give importance to it," says Debi.
- "The world is not going to end if I'm not there," knows Coleman.

Like any balancing act, it's a constant challenge. Michele reminds herself not to get diminishing returns. "Some days are so crazy I'm tempted to skip my workout." That is when she remembers to just put her pencil down. Her priorities are staying fit, family, and work. She knows, "Everybody loses if I lose sight of what is important—especially me."

I was hoping that Chairwoman, who was asked how she keeps a work/life balance, would have looked that woman straight in the eye and said, "My life is my work. That's the balance I have chosen." There's no shame in it, it's not illegal, just own it.

There is an assumption that work/life balance has to be family, friends, neighbors, work, volunteering, stopping global warming. Maybe we just need to pick our priorities for a while and then pick again and then again. I once heard a quote from an elderly woman who said, "I had it all, just not at the same time."

Thermostat Adjustment

Work/life balance? However you define it, it doesn't mean life or work are perfect.

- As you look at all you are juggling, what can you live without for a while?
- Why are you involved in these activities? Is it because you really desire to be involved or because you just aren't too great at saying no?
- How can you wean yourself off the activities that don't matter so much to you right now?
- What would you really like to have in your life, but is missing?
- How can you weave that into your life in a manageable way? What baby steps can you take to begin experiencing that quality or activity?
- What is suffering the most that you really value?

- How can you resuscitate that in your life?
- What do you care about, but now is just not the best timing for it? When would be better? What arrangements can you make now to ensure it reoccurs?

PART III

Cool Off!

Reset the Thermostat

When you are feeling the heat, reset your thermostat and begin lowering the temperature one degree at a time to bring the *real you* back. Make it important to be *you*. Make it a priority to protect, nourish, and sustain your genuine self. Be conscious and alert to the changing circumstances and situations around you. All this takes discipline and courage.

Thrivers have shown us that to keep our frogs hopping, it takes discipline to create experiences every day that feed the soul. It is so easy to let the daily grind sweep us up and take us away.

Who has the energy to take a dance class or join a volleyball team when it takes all we've got to drop the kids off at daycare, go to work, pick the kids up, make dinner, put the kids to bed, and get ready to do it all again the next day? Who has time to think of ways to "add a tiny bit of delight" to the day? You've gotta be kidding! Right? But, by letting the avalanche of responsibilities, demands, and frustrations highjack *you*, you put yourself into the pot to boil one degree at a time.

It takes energy to go with the avalanche *or* to exert the discipline required to be in control, but it's about how you end up. For example, satisfaction and pride in your work is not going to happen by itself. Even people with what you and I may think have great jobs know every job becomes a job.

We need to go deeper inside ourselves and discover ways to feel good about the contribution we make, the experiences we have and create for others, and look to improve what is broken. Once we make that effort, we control the thermostat and open ourselves up to the possibility of being surprised by feeling good about our unique contribution. That sense of satisfaction lowers the temperature in the pot and begins bringing us back to life.

By adding in small ways each day the discipline of managing your finances in a way that keeps you independent and solvent, or resisting the temptation to take the office jerk personally, but instead looking for the person under the monster suit, or to plan little changes in your day, you will start experiencing a fuller self.

But discipline without courage is rowing with one oar. The Thrivers I spoke to, regardless of where they sit in the hierarchy, surprised me with their independent spirit and courage to speak up, step up, and take initiative.

From Ellen putting her head down to fix a bookkeeping system to Paul speaking up to his CEO to Peter making a new habit of inviting people out to lunch to Roger seeking out a relationship with the legal department of his firm, they all opened up their own opportunities to grow and learn about others and themselves in a richer deeper way.

These situations may seem uneventful, but if you look back, you will see each one of these actions took courage. Ellen could easily have just complained about what a lousy bookkeeping system she was stuck with. It wasn't her job to fix it. Think about the moment Paul sat down with his CEO, looked her in the eye, and told her no one trusted her.

Peter could just keep his head stuck in his computer and grab a sandwich by himself. There is always nervousness when calling someone you may not know very well and asking him or her to join you for lunch. "Work life just gets more and more isolating," he says. "But, I always get something out of it even if it's just a new link for good recipes." And how about Roger, do you know anyone who volunteers extra time to help another department?

I've spent fourteen years traveling around the country hanging out with corporate employees talking about how people work together in the workplace. I have learned that cubicle life can be a jungle. There are thousands of moments that are frightening enough to trigger the biological fight-or-flight response or as Paul puts it, "Frightening enough to stop me from being *me*." Coleman remembers always being afraid of getting in trouble, making a mistake, or just looking stupid.

Everybody screws up. It takes courage to own up to mistakes and seek out more information to get a better understanding of how to fix it. It even takes more courage to focus on recovery when someone else makes a mistake. Blaming is a sign of the fight-or-flight response. It is instinctive. Unless you plan to get a lobotomy, it's not going away.

In the jungle, the fight-or-flight response is very effective. It is counterproductive in the office. We need to be alert to and manage our own emotional response and, at the same time, be sensitive that everyone we work with is wired to get defensive, blame, avoid the problem, get frustrated, or withdraw.

We aren't born with discipline and courage any more than we are born with six-pack abs. We are able to develop them. Take your temperature and start chillin'.

Quiz: Take Your Temperature

Is your temperature rising? On a scale of 1 to 5 (as indicated here), please enter the number in the left-hand column that best reflects how strongly you agree with the following statements to take your temperature.

1	2	3	4	5
Strongly Disagree				**Strongly Agree**

—— 1. I dread going to work, but I'm vested; so until I win the lottery, I have to work.

—— 2. It's amazing how one person can make so many people miserable.

—— 3. They (the leadership) are trying to change too much too fast; it's like they're panicking.

—— 4. My manager is just impossible to please.

—— 5. If my personal friends saw me at work, they wouldn't recognize me—I'm different at work.

—— 6. My life is passing me by.

—— 7. I don't even try to address ways to improve things around here anymore; nothing ever changes.

—— 8. It bums me out; I never have time to [fill in with something that fulfills you].

—— 9. Genuineness has been consumed by "political correctness."

—— 10. I keep to myself, you can't trust anyone around here.

—— 11. It feels as if there is a hidden agenda. What management says and what they do don't add up.

—— 12. I never dreamed I'd be doing this for so long.

___ 13. I'm not fooled by what goes on here, I see what they're doing, and some of it is just not right.

___ 14. I often feel tired and annoyed.

___ 15. I am expected to support points of view or actions that don't feel right.

___ 16. It seems someone else is resigning every week.

___ 17. I hear myself saying things or doing things I have despised in others, as if I'm turning into one of "them."

___ 18. I live for the weekends and days off.

___ 19. I don't have time to take care of myself; I've gotten out of shape.

___ 20. I'm tired of hearing myself complain about my job.

___ 21. It kills me to think I'm on this planet to [fill in your job description].

___ 22. I am often anxious about certain individuals at work; they're driving me crazy.

___ 23. I constantly trade off time with family and friends for work stuff, and I've had it!

___ 24. I have perfected my fake laugh.

___ 25. I'm just doing this for the paycheck.

___ 26. More and more is expected of me with no recognition or payoff.

___ 27. I have a hard time focusing and doing my tasks.

___ 28. I find people are often rude and ungrateful.

___ 29. I'm just chasing my tail, not going anywhere.

_____ 30. Nobody understands how much pressure I'm under.

Chillin'

Take your temperature to see how boiled you are, and what is making you hot. Add up your scores in the following table. Circle the totals that are 17 points or more. There may be more than one box. Match that set of numbers with the following common causes for hot water and toss in some ice cubes.

A	B	C
1. _____	2. _____	3. _____
18. _____	4. _____	7. _____
20. _____	10. _____	11. _____
25. _____	16. _____	22. _____
27 _____	26. _____	28. _____
Total _____	Total _____	Total _____
D	**E**	**F**
9. _____	6. _____	5. _____
13. _____	8. _____	14. _____
15. _____	12. _____	19. _____
17. _____	21. _____	24. _____
23. _____	29. _____	30. _____
Total _____	Total _____	Total _____

A: **You're bored.**

Seems obvious, but just by saying it out loud ("Yeah, I'm really bored with my job,") can help gain control over getting some relief. Do you experience any sense of achievement? Are you learning something new or are you stuck in the same ol', same ol'?

Ice cubes:

- Pick something that interests you even slightly at your job or industry and take one action to learn more about it today (check the Internet, the company's intranet, ask people, go to the library, check out different newspaper articles) and do it again for five days. Repeat monthly.
- Choose one thing that needs improvement that is doable and important. Begin learning more about it from different points of view. Come up with a plan to make that improvement and begin building a coalition of support. Set a timeline. Repeat four times a year.
- Add something to your work life: a new connection, new approach to doing your job, new technology, new lunch routine, anything. Repeat this once a month.
- Pick something scary and dive in!

B: **The company/department makes it impossible for you to do your best work.**

Is there is too much bureaucracy? Not enough autonomy? Is the company in trouble? If you are wired for failure either because it's not a right fit or the company is poorly run, you are just killing yourself for nothing.

Ice cubes:

- Make a list of what is specifically getting in the way of doing your best work (often times the things you hear yourself complaining about). Pick the one that is having the most effect on your work and that you have influence or control over. Think of it as if you are the CEO of your company. Looking at it from that point of view, learn more about it by talking to three people from three different angles. Put a plan together to resolve the obstacle and set a timeline. No Debbie Downer talk about how "nothing ever changes."

- From your list, identify the things that are not in your control and will probably never change and accept as many of them as you can and do not put energy into them again.

- If there are things left on that list that you don't have control over and you cannot accept, prioritize getting yourself in a place that suits you better. Give yourself six months.

- Pick something to start doing exceptionally well in spite of the obstacles.

C: You work with a jerk.

We cannot always like everyone we work with, and we undermine career momentum by quitting every time we don't get along with someone we work with.

Ice cubes:

- See this person as a human being (I'm serious), with fears, hopes, and needs. Understand (really understand, from the gut) what it feels like to be him or her. He or she may be doing an Oscar-winning performance of covering it up, but there is humanity there somewhere. Try to find it.
- Identify a character in a book, play, movie, or TV show that reminds you of your jerk. Dwight from *The Office?* Cruella de Vil from *101 Dalmations?*
- Find someone you would prefer to work with and begin heading in that direction by networking and building skills and experience valued by that person.
- Do something to help your jerk succeed in a new and deeper way.

D: **Your personal values are being undermined.**

Are you asked to do/say things or not do/say things that don't feel right, seem unethical?

Ice cubes:

- Make a list of what you feel strongly about.
- Speak up! Be clear about what it is that is making you feel this way and what you need to resolve it. Schedule a lunch or coffee with someone who can influence that aspect of your workplace. Remember these five tips to foster new thinking in discussion:
  - o Acknowledge why you chose them to speak to.
  - o Share your experience and how you feel about the position you are in (without judgment).
  - o Invite the other person to share their experiences and thoughts on the issue.
  - o Initiate a brainstorm of possible solutions.
  - o Thank them for taking the time, for their insights, and for listening to you.
- Be conscious about choices you make that feed your sense of decency and ones that don't. Make the choices that do, don't make the ones that don't. Go back and undo the choices you have made that don't feel right. This may take some time, but that's okay.

- Live your values in everything you do. Give your values top priority. If, like Jeff, pursuing truth is your value, seek the truth, speak the truth, and listen for the truth in everything you do.

E: Your life dreams are suffocating.

Does your workload virtually eliminate the possibility of making progress in your life dreams?

Ice cubes:

- Pick one life dream. Write a few paragraphs describing a moment in your life as if your dream is completely fulfilled beyond what you had imagined.
- Decide to feed your soul by feeding your life dream in small ways. If you want to travel the world in a sailboat, go to a marine store, buy a map or some rope you will need, start charting out your trip. Do one small thing like this once a week.
- Build your Board of Directors for your dream. Make a list of people who have experience, connections, passion, or finances that can support your journey. Take each one out to lunch or meet for coffee to build a closer relationship with them. Find out how you may be able to support them as well.

- Have a visual reminder of your dream in your workplace. If your dream is to be a chef in Italy, change your screensaver to a picture of a Tuscan village. My mother-in-law worked for a motor vehicle department for twenty-five years. She and my father-in-law struggled to make ends meet. She had on her desk a postcard of a beautiful cape house with a picket fence covered with roses. Today that postcard is weathered with age, and they have a beautiful house on Cape Cod with a picket fence covered with roses.

F: **You are part of the problem.**

Come on, somehow you've got to be participating in the problem. Without being clear on how you are contributing to your hot pot, no change will give you lasting relief.

Ice cubes:

- Ask others for candid feedback, then be quiet and listen. Ask people at work, friends, family, anyone, just ask.
  - Ask them what they believe makes you great to work with and what changes would improve how you work with others and how they work with you.
  - Make sure your tone is of genuine curiosity by being genuinely curious.

- o You can ask for clarification. Refrain from saying, "Yeah, but."
- o Share with them your understanding of what they are telling you.
- o Thank them sincerely for their candor.

- Resuscitate yourself with "act as if." Just because you are a nine-to-fiver doesn't mean you cannot experience the life you deserve. Start by acting as if you are living the fullest, coolest life right now. I'm serious. Stop wearing your job like it's sucking the life out of you. Start walking, talking, and acting as if you have it all. Repeat three times a day every day.

- Get a haircut, eat a healthy lunch, take a ten-minute walk, update something in your wardrobe, take a hot bath when you get home, start taking better care of your *self.*

- Lighten up. Be the best CEO (Chief Energizing Officer) for you. Infuse each day with change, learning, passion, playfulness, humor, challenge, and sheer enjoyment of being you in your job. Tolly Burkan, the father of the international firewalking movement, says, "Don't just think out of the box, act out of the box."

Words of Encouragement

Here are a few words of encouragement from some Thrivers:

Rick: "Choose to be in control of your job versus letting it happen to you."

Debi: "Pick a level that will support your lifestyle and be satisfied."

Theresa: "Don't take it too seriously."

Gayle: "Stroke the job, you'll get more back. Behave your way to success."

Cheryl: "Make up your mind."

Paul: "Eat good food and drink good wine."

Coleman: "There is no perfect job. Know what you need most and go for it. I traded security for freedom."

Kathleen: "Keep something for yourself."

Peter: "Think of your workplace as a neighborhood—people."

Carl: "Put your stamp on something."

Patty: "Make a buddy, have a shoulder to cry on when it gets rough."

Carol: "Come into work in a good mood. Expect good luck."

Laurie: "Consciously push your mind out of negativity."

Ellen: "Treat yourself like number one without being selfish."

Siobhan: "Be aware every job has a honeymoon."

Stephanie: "Use downtime wisely."

Michele: "Find an industry you like. Don't be afraid to try a job on for size for a few months before you decide to settle in."

Jill: "Remember who you are and take care of that person."

Steve: "Make a lot of money!"

Appendix

Recommended Books:

- *Work as a Spiritual Practice* by Lewis Richmond

- *Naked at Work (and Other Fears)* by Paul Hellman

- *Love The Work You're With* by Richard Whiteley

- *Goal-Free Living* by Stephen Shapiro

- *The Artist's Way at Work* by Mark Bryan with Julia Cameron and Catherine Allen

- *The Dip: A Little Book That Teaches You When to Quit (and When to Stick)* by Seth Godin

- *Crazy Bosses* by Stanley Bing

- *Happy Hour is 9 to 5* by Alexander Kuerulf

One way to keep cool is to pay attention to what you value and how you spend your time. Here is a quick tool I have created for you to maintain a healthy temperature.

Life Balance Scale

How off kilter is your life? They say people vote with their feet, meaning they show up and spend time doing the things they care most about. But, often times we lose sight of what we value most and end up wasting our lives away doing meaningless things and never showing up to what is most meaningful to us. Step on the Life Balance Scale and fill out the following by giving a score of 1 to 5 for each quality of life for (1) the *time* you spend on it, (2) how much you *value* that quality in your life, and (3) how you assess the *results* you experience in your life.

Life Quality	Time Spent	Value	Results Experienced
Romantic Love Relationship			
Leisure/Down Time			
Family & Friends			
Spirituality			
Physical Fitness			
Career			
Finances			
Life Passion			

What does this mean?

- Take note of the Value column and how the scores relate to the Time column.

  Do you have high scores in the Value column with coordinating low scores in the Time column or vice versa?

  If so, then why are you spending time on things you don't care about and not on things you do?

  Are there any qualities of life you value, but have slid to the back burner?

  Are there any qualities of life that are getting a lot of your time because they were once meaningful, but now that has changed?

- Take note of the Results Experienced column and how your scores coordinate with the Time column.

  Do you have any high scores in the Time column and low scores in the Results Experienced column?

  If so, are there other ways to invest your time more efficiently that will foster better results?

- Take note of the scores in your Value column.

  Are there any qualities that you are overlooking?

  Would you experience gratification if you placed more value on them?

- Take note of your Time column alone.

  Is there a balance of scores?

  Are you spread too thin?

  Are there opportunities to invest your time more wisely?

- Take note of any extremes, either very low scores, or very high scores.

  What do those scores tell you?

  Any surprises?

  Do those scores validate your values?

  Are there alternatives that would align what you really care about and how you spend your time?

Nothing gets us boiling more than conflict with co-workers. Here is a way I have discovered to respond when someone is really posing a challenge that has been a godsend to me in the training room and with colleagues. With some practice, this A.D.V.A.N.S model will help you experience conflict as a way to strengthen understanding and respect.

A.D.V.A.N.S.:
A Way to Cool Off the Emotion in Heated Situations

The workplace is far too emotional to ever expect you are not going to come head-to-head with someone. Most often these situations take us by surprise. Very rarely does anyone send us an e-mail to let us know they are going to challenge our thinking in the middle of our presentation, or cancel an order, or be ticked off at something we said or did. Because it takes us by surprise, it triggers the fight-or-flight response causing us to be defensive or get "caught in the headlights."

How we respond to these situations, particularly in those first few charged moments, determines whether we build a network of trusted colleagues or a world of people who make us uncomfortable. The A.D.V.A.N.S. approach cools off heated interactions by eliminating judgment and fostering an understanding. This allows us to work together against the problem rather than waste energy against each other.

I had a participant in a customer service training a while ago. She was a mutual bond manager. This incident happened during the bond scandal. She and her staff were receiving subpoenas. She was stressed out. She didn't know if she was going to be fired, go to jail, or what! Before 10:00 in the morning, her cell phone went off three times, and she took the calls in the training room. I asked her if it was the best day given she had so many demands outside the classroom. She mumbled how she couldn't turn off her phone and was told she had to take the program and this was the last opportunity. I asked the group if they were going to be okay with it, and they motioned to me just leave her alone as if she might explode.

Well, once we took our morning break, she came barreling up to me livid and blowing my hair back about how unprofessional I was and how I undermined her in front of her staff. Here is the A.D.V.A.N.S. (Allow, Detach, Validate, Ask, Negotiate, and Solve) approach and how it got me through that very heated conversation.

Allow the situation to be as it is. Eckhart Tolle of *The Power of Now* asks, "What is more insane/stupid than to put energy into resisting what already exists?" When someone is challenging you, it takes a counter-intuitive discipline to go to an inner channel to just allow the is-ness. Now, this doesn't mean allow it to continue, just allow that it is, let go of the fight that it shouldn't be. What difference does it make that it shouldn't be? It is. Being able to switch from defensiveness to *allow* cleanses your body language, including your facial expressions and tone of voice from any judgment. This is a step done from within, and it sets the tone for the rest of the interaction.

When this mutual bond manager was screaming at me, of course, at first I wanted to either run away crying or throw her to the floor, put my foot on her chest, and rubber neck her! I mean, geez, who lets their cell phone go off three times in a training program *and* takes the call? Instead, I went to *allow,* and when I did, she became a very stressed out, scared, out-of-control person. I began to feel a little sorry for her.

D*etach* from the situation personally. Take yourself out of it. Detach from the outcome. Let go of what might happen or not happen or what someone might think or not think. Detaching from the situation opens the mind and the capacity for empathy.

As I said, I began to feel a little sorry for this bond manager. I detached from it being about what I did or didn't do to trigger her response, or how I might be judged as a facilitator by the other participants and the client. I just unplugged all that thinking and became very present in the moment.

Validate your understanding of the other person's point of view. This doesn't mean you agree with their point of view or are apologizing or saying you understand, it's putting into your own words how you are understanding what they are telling you.

Once I was able to allow this situation to be, detach from it personally, I began to listen empathetically, and without even thinking about it, I found myself saying, "And that's the last thing you needed today." Her whole demeanor completely diffused and she said, "Yeah, tell me about it." At that moment it went from being us against each other to us against the problem.

Ask for more information to deepen your understanding of the whole situation and its complexities. Now that you have allowed the situation to exist without judgment, and detached from it personally triggering empathy, your tone of voice will resonate with genuine curiosity. This is critical particularly in the asking stage because if you are still feeling defensive or angry, your questions may sound condescending or sarcastic.

I asked the bond manager what she would have preferred me to do. She said I should have called a break and spoken to her privately. I agreed. I wish it occurred to me in the moment.

Negotiate what you can begin doing or stop doing and what the other person can do or not do to direct the situation toward a resolution. Often, we skip to this stage prematurely. By establishing a mutual understanding and respect through the first four steps, the quality of the negotiation is genuine and collaborative.

It was silent between us for a moment. I asked, "Is there anything I can do now to make it okay for you to return?" She and I realized it was unrealistic for her to continue in the program given the crisis she was dealing with.

Solve the problem. A true resolution in these situations is gained when all parties have contributed in some way to creating the solution. Be deliberate to create a collaborative spirit by asking for their views, ideas, and concerns.

It made sense for the bond manager to miss the customer service training, but she did come to the managing customer service program. I enjoyed her full participation. She was very animated and thoughtful in the small and large group activities. Her cell phone never peeped.

You may be thinking, "Hey, she was rude, she should have apologized to you and the other participants!" True. She could have acknowledged the position she put me in. She didn't. So what? By coming to my next program and being such a contributor was her way of saying she would have liked to have acted differently as well. I have found results are more important than "being right."

Made in the USA
Middletown, DE
10 April 2018